ANTHONY WILSON

FULL STRETCH

Poems 1996 – 2006

ACKNOWLEDGEMENTS

Thanks are due to the editors of the following publications in which some of these poems, or earlier versions of them, first appeared: *The Argotist Online*, *Catalogue 2002-2003* (Worple Press), *English in Education*, *Exeter Flying Post*, *Maquette Magazine*, *The Rialto, Seam, Smiths Knoll, The Tall Lighthouse Poetry Review*, *Third Way*, *Warp and Weft* (Worple Press, 2006).

'The Surprise' was commissioned by *Ways With Words Literature Festival* and was published in *Poems Inspired by the Dartington Hall Gardens* (The Droridge Press, 2005).

'Forgiveness' was read in *Sowing Seeds for Life*, a service celebrating the 150th Anniversary of St Luke's College, at Exeter Cathedral.

Poems from Part Two appeared in *Nowhere Better Than This* (Worple Press, 2002); some of these were previously published in *The Difference* (Aldeburgh Poetry Trust, 1999). Poems from Part Three appeared in *How Far From Here Is Home?* (Stride, 1996). Some minor alterations have been made to the text of some of these poems.

'Post-Op' appeared in the *Independent on Sunday*.

For their friendship and advice I am grateful to Andy Brown, Peter Carpenter, Joanna Cutts, Siân Hughes, Naomi Jaffa, Michael Laskey, Henry Shukman, Jean Sprackland and the South West Writers Group. Thank you Em for the typing.

For how could he explain to them what it meant to be a writer...
a world that was entirely different,
and yet it would include the sofa
and the smell of chicken cooking

— Louis Simpson

CONTENTS

I
FULL STRETCH

Seeing it Through

II
FROM NOWHERE BETTER THAN THIS

III
FROM HOW FAR FROM HERE IS HOME?

for Tatiana, Merenna and Shimi

I
FULL STRETCH
NEW POEMS

Your daughter's tall

— Thomas Lux

A PAUSE FOR THOUGHT

The way it takes us, unbidden and unhurried:
the moment's pause outside a tunnel
or when men on allotments stretch between spadefuls,
noticing that hours have passed like days in grief,
the time with nothing to show the world
except the weight of thoughts we did not know
as 'thoughts' but impressions we might one
day push into use, in jokes or conversation,
or in letters to friends in need of persuading
we exist but not in the way they remember.

It is like growing old, or suddenly knowing
we could have, should have, done better
with what we had, or our sense of it at least,
whatever was right or planned, wherever it took us.

NOWHERE YOU KNOW

It is nowhere you know, or claim to.
If pushed, you might say you grew up there
and left quickly, or knew someone
with its accent at university
who didn't cope but couldn't go back.

Looking no different to the place
you know and love, this is where careers
mire in scandal or booze, or rocket,
fuelled by ambition and luck,
target of theme pubs, chain stores, young Turks.

In its terrified parishes
churchwardens stare into tea served by wives
whom fashion has forgotten,
their sons and daughters all gone,
their letters rebutting the tide of ideas.

Its park-keepers and poets squabble
over crumbs of government funding, the rubble
of used-up favours and affairs
like league tables the real world ignores.
Its football team flirts with mediocrity.

Visit and you'll recognise
its roundabouts sponsored by solicitors;
its business park with motorway links;
its historic this, that and the other attracting
mystified tourists at teahouses.

If you stay you'll notice how jokes
about accents from other towns,
like excuses for trains being late,
are those you've already made habit,
in your own time and voice.

THE SURPRISE
for Andy Brown

A cranefly struggling
through sodden grass,

an upturned bee
on your windowsill;

stars close enough
to touch and you

a six-year-old,
transfixed —

like the rhyme whispered
by the beech hedge —

reminding
that what passes

(candlelight; laughter; dew;
sheep in the field next-door)

is what's loved well;
this evening solid

as jet trails you marvel at
on waking,

or lawn-stripes caught
from upstairs rooms,

holding yourself
for warmth, your life

a garden bench left out,
facing all weathers.

SLEEP MACHINE

And you have watched
              your own hands
melt before your eyes
              children weeping at airports
stones   pictures of stones
              screaming under the sun
dawn-break
              and nightfall
windy platforms
              torrents of leaves spinning
then falling while you fall
              into the arms of your father

Or you veer
              off the road into a tree
with flowers
              already strapped to it
your son slips headfirst
              off the jetty
no one in the auditorium
              your briefcase empty
you kiss
              a woman
you have never met
              the doctor says it is bowel cancer

In June heat *Othello*
              or the African Clawed Toad
erase themselves
              like a virus in the film
of the spy   all that's left
              your breathing
and a quote on your left hand
              in smudged biro   Queen Victoria
or Elizabeth
              looking herself in the mirror
after the news
              declaring   Today I will be good

THE REPRIEVE

And ride again
        by the river
               with Shim

of a Saturday
        trying to spot
               the heron

or pause
      by the skate-park
             to gawp

at parabolas
        or glimpse
              a late try

on marigold pitches
           or when frozen
                  at Exmouth
a flask
    is passed round
            all I offer

    is 'Thanks'

SPINACH

The doctors don't know why.
'It literally means thinning of the bone,'
they smile. 'What is your calcium
intake like? Don't just think of cheese,
several vegetables are good, like spinach.
What about your family history?'

'My back obeys what my family history
tells it to,' I reply. 'I've no idea why,
but I've never liked spinach.'
I only ever broke one bone.
My favourite meal has to be cheese
fondue. I know the code for calcium

but seem to have trouble absorbing calcium
like a general ignoring history
marching troops on bread and cheese.
I lie awake sometimes trying to figure why
I am so worried about my bones
or whether to take up eating spinach,

though frankly the thought of spinach
makes me want to retch. Trapping calcium
seems as much fun as snapping bones
or failing 'O' level History
on your own, to which you moan 'Why
me?', while the rest tut 'Hard cheese'.

If my bones don't get me, the cheese
will, I'm sure. I look up spinach
recipes in a panic, forgetting why
I need to watch my calcium,
what it tastes like, or what history
might have to say about loss of bone

in men under forty, who did not bone
up their science, who know cheese
goes well with red (but not its history),
that we'd be safer chewing spinach
for our daily dose of calcium.
Not one doctor can explain to me why

on this day in history I have to rely on spinach
to stop my bones turning soft like cheese.
'It's all to do with calcium,' they say, but do not know why.

INQUISITION

The weak and infirm,
did you heal them?

The beggar growling
at your gates,
did you kiss his wounds?

Those speeches you gave,
their syntax like a mask,
were you sure
they would save us?

What did you think
our weeping meant,
meeting after meeting:
that our scribblings
were notes on your sermons,
not the absurd doodles
of the condemned?

When did you touch us?
When did you feed us?

As news of your triumphs
crossed the parishes,
how did you sleep?

The gale of your edicts
lashed our cottages:
did a smile crack your lips?

Repeat after me:
I ached for you to join us
as we built our temple of fire.

THE MEETING STARTED WITH PRAYER

And the Procedures were read out.
Any woman 'with the curse' was to leave immediately,
and those with child or suspected of being so.
Women who stayed were to remain silent.
Men who worked with their hands
were to speak only when prostrate
before the Leader, facing the floor.
Men in suits could speak uninterrupted
after making their cash donation.
Men in workmen's boots, men carrying children
and men sporting adornments of any kind
were to give their address at the door.
Motions to vote could be moved through the Chair
but only when prompted by The Frog
and only when the Chair concurred that The Frog had indeed spoken.
If the motion was not deemed Frog-inspired
all record of it would be destroyed by fire.
Members were reminded that The Frog had not spoken
for over two thousand years.
The Minutes of the previous meeting were approved.
There were no Matters Arising.

FORGIVENESS

for John and Elizabeth Searle

Their eyes bloom at the story.
'The roof was caked mud and straw
so it would have hurt their hands.
They lowered the man down slowly
to where Jesus stood talking with his friends.'
The deliberate drone of my voice stumbles
on that final demand to *Take
up your mat and walk*: 'Can you tell back
what happened?' As faces bend parallel
to paper there's a silence I'm not sure
I've earned, perhaps like the cripple that day,
shaky of the trust shown in him.
As they swarm by the door to go home
I see him sprinting the same, punching the sky.

SALAD DRESSING

To make a vinaigrette
such as angels

would kill for
you need first pressing

virgin oil balanced
by cider vinegar;

salt and pepper to taste;
the opaque swirl of Dijon.

For sweetness
some add a dab of honey,

a sprinkle of caster
from an heirloom.

Throw in a fistful
of chives for extra bite.

To give it real fire
add a pinch of cayenne, Lea and P.

Forget young shoots
and stirring from the bottom

of the bowl. Drizzle it
into his navel

till his stomach
becomes a lake.

Now go under,
drinking deep,

your face rising
like a mud-mask.

Swallow everything.
Believe what you eat.

FOR PETER BOURKE
AFTER WATCHING HIM PLAY CLOV

The Gospel choirs and evangelists
were in good voice

as I walked to the tube,
the night of the fifteenth World Cup

Final, a *dénouement* of blistering negativity
between Italy

and Brazil,
Baggio cancelling Romario, the existential

burden of not losing
crushing *the beautiful game.* Your timing,

Peter, was sharper —
I never saw you work harder

at not being jolly.
What I'll take with me

is you rooted
motionless at the end,

unable to pick up your
suitcase and staring into the ether

as a 'keeper might, the eternity
of extra-time a memory

blotted out now it's penalties, the first
shot and every one after it sudden death.

Seeing it Through

SEEING IT THROUGH

After the disbelief, the phone calls at all hours,
the facts persist:
he'd planned it a while,
the cupboards empty
but for a tin of sardines.

What else remains is this:
four days before, he gossiped late
about a poet;
two days before deleted a comma;
the day itself washed up, left a note to feed the cats.

THE BOOT

I found the boot on the bandstand:
brown leather, laceless,
daylight showing through the sole,
yellow mud in the heel-grips;

inside a metal toy Mercedes,
blue, with doors that opened,
a bitten-off black fingernail
reclining on the back seat.

SNOWBALL

for Martin

And I never wore an anorak.
I never even left the kitchen.
There were no stones to throw,
not in those days.

So I never was in that garden.
The snow covered the tracks
I did not make,
dreaming of thaw.

BEACH

We struggle to stay upright on the shingle.
The wind bangs the umbrella so we bellow
above each other's sense of where it all went wrong:
my throwing up in the bar, your useless directions.

As I stumble back, the idea takes you
then your clothes. You collapse into the blackness
with a crash. You plunge away from me
giggling, kicking glitter in your wake.

WE DO NOT TOUCH

We do not touch for months.
We lie reading with our books
then whisper goodnight to the ceiling
worrying about tomorrow.

Lying reading with our books
we tunnel through others' lives,
their worries about tomorrow
like far off planets

or tunnels in others' lives
we catch the tremors from.
Like far off planets
they glimmer a moment, then fade.

We catch the tremors from
their sadness and their joy
which glimmer a moment, then fade,
forgotten conversations.

Your sadness and my joy
— polar opposites we share —
are forgotten conversations
we carry with us, into day.

Polar opposites, we share
but do not touch for months.
We carry each other into day
by whispering goodnight to the ceiling.

ON WHITE HILL

We lay down together
in the tall bracken,
out of view of the hill-farm,
below the quad-track

to Addison Moss,
in sight of the fort,
its ditches like ripples,
the shepherd's hut

chimneys two staring
ewes on the next ridge
where a Harrier
once materialised

through its roar
shaking owl pellets
from the dyke
and us to our core.

AFTER THE FUNERAL

She found: a transistor tuned to the football,
a mirror nailed to the ceiling,
a blow-up mattress and foot-pump,
enough Pirelli posters to start a garage

and curled into his wellies a selection
of Page Threes rolled up like truncheons —
for starting bonfires, she assumed, soaking
them in his last jamjar of creosote.

LEARNING TO CYCLE

As you fade and fade across the park
something in me cracks:
the thought that one day
you won't need me for a thing,
not even my applause or praise,
or pointing out how upright you are sitting.

MY THIRTIES

Decade of my last exam and first child
I say goodbye to you as to a house-guest
who came to stay a week, then seemingly forever,
his red shirt sending the white wash pink.

I sail away from you, an island I visited
without learning the language or impressing
the well-shod natives who ate only barbecued
chicken with expensive German wine.

I see you as a party I left just after
midnight, hoping I did not slur drunkenly
at the woman I wanted to flirt with, who,
it turns out, had plans to leave with me anyway.

TO DO LIST

I do not want to die completing you.
Your shirt-tugging appals me,
your whining, off-stage,
like a dentist's drill,
shears the last seconds
of the Gaugin-girl singing ecstatically.

You, with your laundry,
tax, the fence,
your jottings strangle my attention.
I write to Peter because I need to,
not because you said.
Whoosh! go the childhoods of my children.

Unread books, friendships I lose
through tiredness, do you bless them?
Or that boy peering
round the curtain at the log-farm?
Or that woman smiling to herself
in the rain, her face lit up like an angel?

WHEN THE HOLY SPIRIT
DANCED WITH ME IN MY KITCHEN

the first thing I noticed was his arms,
thick and hairy like a bricklayer's
with a tattoo of an anchor
as Churchill had.

'Coming for a spin?' he grinned,
in an accent more Geordie than Galilee,
and he whirled me
through tango, foxtrot and waltz
without missing a beat.

'You're good,' I said. 'Thanks,'
he said, taking two glasses to the tap.
'You're not so bad yourself,
for someone with no sense of rhythm
and two left feet.'
He gave me a wink.

'It's all in the waist.
The movement has to start there
or it's dead.'

'You'll find it applies to most things,'
he went on, grabbing the kettle.
'Writing, cooking, kissing,
all the things you're good at,
or think you are.'
He winked again.

'You don't mind me asking,' I said,
'but why are you here?'
                              'I thought it was about time,'
he said. 'I mean, you've been full stretch,
haven't you, what with your job,

feeling like a taxi for the kids,
your family living far away,
and you 'in your head' all the time
as you said to someone last week.'

I looked at him and nodded.
                              'Go on.'
'I was going to.'
He got down some mugs.
'Let's say I was concerned about you.
The thing is, the three of us,
we like you a lot.
We think you've got real potential
as a human. You're kind and humorous.
You're also a little scatty.
We like that. By the way, that fish curry
you made on Saturday was first class.'

'You know about that?'
'Everything you get up to,'
he smiled. 'It's nothing to panic about.
Really. To tell you the truth
you could do with loosening up a little.
Try not beating yourself up the whole time.
A little less rushing everywhere
would do you good, too.'

'I thought you might say that.'
                    'Look at me,' he said.
'I came to say:
Keep Going, and Relax.
Also: keep things simple.
If you are doing one thing,
do that thing. If you are talking

with someone, listen to them,
do not blame them for being hard work.
Write as if you were not afraid,
and love in this way too.
Be patient with everyone, especially
your relations, who (I can assure you)
think you are rather special.
Make big decisions slowly, and small decisions
fast. Do not make bitterness your friend.
Pray (I will not mind if you use
made up words for this.)
Garrison was right: 'Why
have good things you don't use?'
What you have been given to do,
give yourself to it completely,
only by emptying yourself can you become full.'

THE EXETER POETS

- how far away is Leicester?

Spike Milligan

There are eleven of us in all.
I am eighth best,

after Rupert the most shaven-headed,
the best-looking after Andy,

whose coffee is stronger than mine.
Technically Lawrence is my neighbour.

He is actually round the corner,
the best at talking to my kids.

Chris does not live in Exeter, but works here,
so is one, plus we all adore him.

He is the most scientific, sometimes, and theological.
I live for those moments he winces

over verbs and line-endings, his famous
'Chinese assassin' face heralding pain.

Hilary and Candy are Totnes poets
and may outstrip us all: it is up to them.

James gives the longest introductions;
the other James gives even longer ones.

We are not a 'community', nor, yet, 'a sack of vipers',
still less a 'school'. Ann is the best poet for miles

around Liskeard, including Plymouth.
I last saw Alexis at the station.

When I said I was heading for London he looked disappointed.
He is reading next week at the Black Box

(a deathly venue, why do we put up with it?)
To get into the top seven I may need

to construct an epic from old SAAB manuals
or copies of the *Express and Echo*. Or revamp

my 83 two-line poems 'On my Baldness'.
Chris will hate it, but then he is top six

so has nothing to worry about,
up there on the Moor with its ponies and sky.

PEOPLE IN THE LIFE

Yesterday it was the swimming kit,
today the letter about homework.

We argue while we walk; Vaughan smiles
they are flying to Cork.

'You are no longer my friends.'
Yes, I will put your clothes away

and talk to Keith about the fennel.
Bruce says the days shorten faster

past forty. Frances is in Dublin, shopping.
Penny says we don't see you.

Last evening I picked up the carpet fluff.
I missed a management meeting, but not

with my soul. Wayne read powerfully
at the Cabaret.

My name was not on the posters.
I should have asked I suppose.

'Domesticity is my forte,
as abstraction longs to be yours.'

Late (again) at home-time
Jonathan looked very dischuffed.

His eyes are the darkest since Jane's.
On the radio African children in harmony

reducing most theory to rubble.
'Wagner understood how to tell stories.'

Come back, Wayne, we miss your poems
and shirts. Einstein was dyslexic,

as was Agatha Christie, who is read,
they say, continuously

round the globe aboard aircraft,
their jet trails like scratches in a windscreen.

LENT

I have finished my chapter for Judith.
I celebrate in the usual way

by logging on to Amazon
to buy one of Naomi's recommendations.

I know the publisher
but have not skied with him. Yet.

In the three-week wait
for it to arrive

I try to live without coffee,
crabby with the children,

unrecognisable to myself and my wife
even during lovemaking.

Distance
can be habit-forming.

As we arrived outside Hawick
we put on a Romantic duets CD

and argued about 'Endless Love'.
The Plough looked touchable

above Ewart's farm,
the moon a half-eaten egg.

RAY

The first book of Ray's I bought was *Fires*, in
Northwood. For two weeks I got up early,
reading chunks in the bookshop, loving his
no-nonsense tone, the way such simple words
could take your breath away: 'writers sometimes
need to stand and gape at this or that thing
— a sunset or old shoe — in simple joy.'

It is hardly new to say Ray's poems
are plain, but it was this, in Babel's words,
which pierced my heart like a full stop placed
precisely. This was the first time I'd seen
writerly behaviour made flesh: hanging
cards with quotes above the desk; borrowing
from everyday events and speech, a wrong
number dialled at midnight for example.

His account of watching laundrette drums spin
kids' clothes one Saturday in Iowa
gripped me. He knew there and then, he says,
that nothing would shape his writing like they.
This cut through me when I had kids myself:
one storm-wracked night in Penzance I drove ink-
wet streets to quiet my son, saw the gale
abate and knew I'd have to keep things brief.

I turn to *Fires* most often, as one does
a favourite pair of jeans or coffee brand;
sometimes as homage; and for instruction.
The first time I finished it I knew life
had turned suddenly, as his best friend says.
'Nothing, it seemed, would ever be the same.'

Or this one: overheard in a pub
or from a friend, whose friend of a friend
it was, their eyes wide with it.
A couple (you might even know them)
try for years for a baby. They re-mortgage,
sell the car, change diet. The doctors
implore them to stop. One morning
on the scales she's two pounds heavier.
Or this (it could be the same couple).
They've sold the car (they walk to work anyway)
but give it one last shot on the drugs.
A boy, beautiful, just like his father, tight curls.
Three years later the last roll of the dice
brings triplets, all girls. They visit many
car showrooms. Or this. They try for years:
nothing. Take half a pill: twins. Then twins
the next year, no pill involved. Or this.
Triplets; then twins, after the vasectomy.
Or: the sour-faced man who tells everyone
he's done, one daughter is enough.
One day she tells him everything,
including about the needle and the condom.
What do you imagine he feels then?

HELLO HOME

hello front door and hall and hall table with two coins
and a postage stamp hello stairs that stain will have
to go hello mail-pile with your two-week-old news
hello kitchen you smell stale hello pot plants
I warned you didn't I? hello window onto the garden
and newly asphalted guinea-pig hutch for which
not one word of thanks hello washing machine
yes I did need all those T shirts hello red bill
you got me again hello postcard from Cornwall
our was too hello kettle hello teapot hello shop
with your milk and local paper hello Roy no I didn't
know that hello chair you still hurt my back
hello suitcase which market were *these* from?
hello drawers hello wardrobe hello fleece behind
the bedroom door hello bathroom did she clean like
she promised? hello mirror not bad for Scotland
hello uncomplaining toiletries hello hairbrush
it's been a while hasn't it? hello phone ringing already
hello 25 messages blinking hello I bought you this
hello thanks for coming with me

The kitchen swells with music,
or as Mike says, whales,
while the others go through beauty routines.
I bring mail to the table
girdled by one red elastic band
and start sifting,
ripping the plastic wrapping
from mail order catalogues, deciding against
a yellow Prince of Wales check shirt
but ticking a toolkit for the car.
Next door's cat arches her back
on our shared wall
and is silhouetted marvellously
against the colour-filling sky,
one tentative paw placed after another,
a scent, perhaps, making her pause,
or our nodding back door jasmine,
its shadows trying to harden.
There are little spots of grease showing
on the white bread-bag. I pull
off one wheat grain from the crust
and try to chew it, harder,
at this hour, than concrete.
In the paper, an interview
with a Turkish émigré
smiling stiffly in his portrait
as though recently recruited
to some backwoods university.
There is a perfect circle of mould,
no bigger than a fingernail,
on the nectarine in front of me.
Is it warm enough to risk shoes without socks?
In a second Ruth will be here
for Shim. Which leads me
to the gorgeousness of this late March day,

sun against the blue,
branches swaying nearly green,
all of it tense, somehow,
yet charged with appetite, too.
Plus the thought that Naomi's poems
are similarly gorgeous, more full, now,
of beauty times pain divided by joy,
a cause to celebrate,
like this morning, the roses waving
Goodbye in their vase,
the daffodils nodding Hello Sexy in theirs,
pans awaiting scrubbing
and the page the pencil, like this day,
this gift of a day,
in which there will be chance conversations
with neighbours, planned repartee
with artists who earn their living by other means,
coffee, Chelsea winning away
and attention later to what Palace might do
such is my love of Peter and John
and my liking of Tim
who told me to get my haircut in the first place.
Even the ketchup bottle,
so normally sturdy and unflappable,
lets out a gasp, sleep falling
from its eyes, the better to look with.

FROM A SAVER RETURN

for Peter and Amanda Carpenter

This is where it ends:
the one-hour wait at Maidenhead;
messages from three days
like two weeks' worth.

What do we want
as we stare at the countryside?
Sunlight, strong coffee, the paper;
our talk remembered like whisky.

What I miss already
is what we left unsaid:
a barge pulling through lock gates
vanishing as we charge this tunnel.

II

FROM NOWHERE BETTER THAN THIS

Just as there is a toilet in every house,
There is a lunchbox of dung in every man

— Yorifumi Yaguchi

JOURNEY

It is dusk in Wiltshire.
Pausing for a change of guard at Westbury
I can just about make it out
on the escarpment. Not prehistoric
or Roman, nineteenth century probably,
is given a new coat each May.
The suit opposite doodles next to the crossword,
the quick one, in red biro. The bar shut
for ten minutes at Reading and hasn't reopened.
With conversation more risky than poetry
I decide against asking him if I sleeptalked,
though want to, so strong was my impression
of you next to me, then above me.
In the queue behind a broken down freight
outside Bristol there's a chance to admire
who Brunel was: a genius, at twenty three,
cutting west through hillsides, rock,
woods rising sheer from the track.
With the light properly fading at Taunton
a gun dog crashes after a rabbit,
the pleased angle of a twelve bore, smoking open.
Tell me, is this what success is:
to spend more time away from home trying
to avoid the eye of the woman
with the beige T-shirt and improbable breasts,
and concentrate instead on the motorway,
now parallel with us, a herd of Friesians
inching towards the corner of a field,
a barge following its ripple
and this taxi to this door which in September
I will be putting down as expenses.

WE ARE SITTING IN THE BLUE PASSAT ESTATE

but we will not buy it.
It stinks of dogs for one thing (Labradors,
at a guess) and the spec is really poor.
Sure it's got windows, sunroof
and a boot the size of Alaska
but the miles are wrong side of 65
and for a K that's bargepole territory. Colour
isn't great, but never as bad as
that silver diesel saloon on Marsh Barton
with the hole in the carpet, one careful
chain-smoking rep, an L at only 795.
Peter's moustache spies what we don't,
though, that he's got us already: despite
our practised jargon
we can't tell brake fluid from water.
By letting us drive this crapheap
the three miles to Broadclyst
he knows we'll want something better,
that other one, terrific value, twelve hundred more
and burgundy which he'll persuade us
is 'Indian red', and rare.
By the time I write him my cheque
I don't care about full history or even
that BT owned it first: it'll get us to the Borders,
and maybe next year Lausanne
where it will stick out in the car park
to my aunt's flat as German with a Britannia Ferries
GB sticker next to its Top Marks
number plates spelt with a 'que' for a joke.

LEAVING BRIXTON

It's summer and we are living in a house
we don't own. We hang washing in the garden,
carry trays with salad and wine from the kitchen
which feels too small, and slump in front of the news

as we used to, at home, but it doesn't feel right.
The railway keeps us awake
long after we've finished worrying about
who we'll stay with next.

When your park-trip with the kids
didn't work out this morning
I kept one, you took one, and I read
to him, then fed him, then put him

down, then fed him again, his eyes closing and closing.
They looked brown. Last time they were green.
When was the last time I looked? — It's gone.
I need to be homeless more often.

WHAT THEY LEFT BEHIND

Two pallets, wooden,
one mattress, double and damp,
a police cone, a roll of carpet,
blue, threadbare and sodden,
a floodlight minus sensor,
a bucket of ashes, soot
halfway across the sitting room
floor, a chest of drawers
with THIS IS CRAP LEAVE IT
in red felt tip on a sticker,
the kitchen sink (a surprise)
and keys to the back door.

In the garden a T.V. aerial,
two iron bedsteads tangled
with bindweed, ivy,
a strimmer with a coil
of green wire, a spare key
under a stone, a toilet cistern
(with parts), a hubcap, Italian,
and a dead car battery.
In the loft twelve cardboard
boxes, one too big for the hatch,
and a lightbulb, 60 watt, the one
they forgot to take with them.

LOGGING

Yesterday I went logging with Jock.
Me chopping, him stacking between cigarettes.
We talked about books, about moving, our children.
He described it to me as Zen,
how if you visualise the axe splicing the log
it becomes an act of deliverance, faith even.
How the rhythm can become you over time,
the desire not to lose it palpable, like sweat.
This evening I was out there on my own.
I thought how odd, a Catholic
and a Protestant divining manual labour as Zen.
Both struggling, both with boulders from childhood,
the long silence of the cup rising to the lips.
But we'd worked well together, no question.
By the time he took up the chopping
a pile was already growing, me stooping
to pick up a couple each time he paused,
and fling them flat and fast, like Frisbees,
some spinning as if to fly half, breaking out of defence.
Some I didn't even watch where they landed.
There were two logs I just couldn't do.
All the Zen in the world wouldn't crack them.
Too knotted. I left them to the frost.

The night before my father would lay out
on his side of the bed wallet, camera, maps,
francs, washbag and passports,
meticulous as an assassin. Downstairs
my mother hissed at the kitchen floor.

At five the next morning her hand wobbled on your shoulder
and we sleepwalked through clothes to the car.
Breakfast was cornflakes on the beach at Dover,
and grit in marmalade sandwiches.
And there'd be a photograph. Nobody spoke.

On the ferry you could want to die.
We'd huddle on deck with thermos and anoraks
while my father unfurled a map deploying us
like tentpegs in a groundsheet.
We churned an unrelenting wake of Englishness.

France was always *too hot* and lunch was horseflies
and sunburn. Once we parked next to the Metro.
Speaking through my mother at the gendarmerie
my father didn't flinch when he listed as the contents
of his suitcase *twelve ties*. It was the maps he missed.

You woke next morning to scooters in alley ways
and women in slippers and dressing gown staggering
under baguettes. Coffee. A man cursing his car.
(This could be Dijon, Lyons or Besançon.)
We slept badly because the pillows were *like rocks*.

Then that last leg through Pontarlier and the hills.
The highest big town in Europe, boys, the clouds
like a lake in the valley. Finally a door opened
and a new accent would start. My mother ceased translating.
The welcome we had walked into flew straight over our heads.

THE WALLET MY GRANDFATHER GAVE ME

is in use again. For ten years
it's rested in my desk drawer,
put into retirement by the one you bought me on Skiathos.
We lay on the roof and undressed each other.

I was hearing voices in those days,
would have gone mad without you.
Goat bells in the mists of the olive groves.
The first time I ever swam naked.

The day it went into the drawer
I pulled out of it your photograph
and a ticket to a place called Hildenborough,
cardboard, stiff, a single.

IN THE BRETHREN

Dad, what am I doing here?
What is it I am doing now?
Are you proud of me?

— W.S. Graham

The cough-thick silence
put everyone in their place.

We were told:
If you speak, make sure you speak to God.

If you were a child you could not speak.
If you were a lady you could not speak.

When I first spoke I heard
my voice say ' — and Jesus still loved

Peter. He took him in his arms
and forgave him as a father would his

son.' Outside your hand tensed on my shoulder.
'You showed great insight in there.

Well done.' I stood there
renewed and released, your hoped-for

unimagined blessing
shocking

me into places
where church could not go. Let differences

be differences.
Likenesses, likenesses. Wrap me up in your arms.

MEMBURY

Was the hour-mark from home,
its guy-roped radio mast visible five minutes away,
on winter nights an eye-sized ember blinking at its tip.

Membury, where the wind off the plain is a knife,
petrol-outpost for the desperate, coffee-refuge
for men sitting singly outstared by their reflections;

where we never stopped, not even to pee or for gum,
place-between, time-point, neither family nor school,
our conversation eddying as your wedding ring

tapped Telemann on the steering wheel,
the miles charging by in a blur of furrows and sheep.
Did you know where you were driving us?

— Not only to masters who taught you,
the ancient hunger and cold, but cigarettes fumbled
in bushes, madness and stealing towels,

boys being kicked downstairs, kicked for crying,
kicked to stop them phoning home?
None of us kept a diary.

On clear nights at Membury we gazed into that
and said nothing. I can see you refuelling
with apple pie on the way back, toying, as you pull out,

with picking up that hitcher who reminds you
of your son. If I was that hitcher now I'd ask
Take me back to Membury. Buy me a coffee and we'll talk.

I AM BECOMING MY DAD

The way I let coffee grow cold,
build skyscrapers of bills on my desk,
and will look at a map only once
especially when lost. I catch him
in my *Well done* to their pictures
and needing to beat them at Memory.

Never knowingly wrong,
I'll argue the semantics of 'going to'
for an hour. Like him, I buy
only one brand of red, am faithful
to the same pair of brogues,
resoling them before weddings.

Twins in edginess during rugby
we love Bond films, keep cheque book
stubs, would kill for a fry up.
My sister says I've inherited
his trouble with piles. Unlike him,
I can't tell if she's serious.

MY FOX

after Raymond Carver

A fox came into my garden.
Not Aesop's, or Chaucer's,
or the fox of William Shakespeare.
Nor Ben Jonson's, nor that of Dr Seuss.
It was unlike most foxes that you see
in that it looked like a fox.

It was not Ted Hughes' fox
who had made plans to go fishing that day
but found himself instead on the point
of being torn to shreds by a pack of baying hounds;
it was not Philip Larkin's fox:
the view of a cemetery at 3 o'clock in the morning
in the rain
disguised as a fox;
it was not Seamus Heaney's fox
which had lain buried for centuries
under a pub in West Belfast
and so knew a thing or two about life as a fox,
so well preserved were his faculties;
nor was this laughing Sam Beckett's fox
who had no arms and no legs and no tail
and who lived in a dustbin on a dungheap
playing chess with its snout
against no-one
but who was reputedly one of the most cheery foxes the sun ever
blessed
with its rays;
nor was it that nice Ezra Pound's fox,
created in part from the bones of other foxes
and whom fox-hunters everywhere respected
but never really as it were admitted to *liking*;
nor was it T.S. Eliot's fox
in the garden

63

the garden
the garden before dawn
the eternal dawn before time
when History is Now and the Fox;
and it was not Wallace Stevens' fox
which was really thirteen different foxes
each of them nothing to do with being a fox;
it was not the fox in translation,
a cunning ruse of a metaphor
smuggling dissent into the minds of the proletariat
against state control over aspects of daily life such as
chicken coops, wire fencing and hunting laws;
nor was it even Raymond Carver's fox
which did its best to act like a regular fox
but had in fact just left his wife
and developed a drink problem:

no. It was none of these foxes.
It was a fox. I mean — it was a fox.
It stood still for a second, listening, in my garden.
It had a scar on its left flank.
Then it walked, like a fox walks, silently out of my life.

LEONARD COHEN IS MY BARBER

He works at Tony's, Northcote Road,
three doors down from the bookshop,
backwater of antiques and health food.

He isn't the owner, though could be,
if he wanted, preferring to hover at No.3,
'the quiet one' in the corner by the door,

his conversation elegant and clipped,
never far from remembrance or prayer.
We nod at each other like accomplices

and he beckons me to my chair.
He vanishes a second from the mirror
adorned with *Babes of New York*

and *Five Views of Cyprus* postcards
as he flicks the cape out in front of me.
His fingers tuck in the tissue,

their whiff of Marlborough and aftershave
knowing what I want already —
No. 2 round the sides and back

and the best he can do with the top.
I want to ask about Marianne,
Janice and Kris, about unmade beds,

raincoats and dockyards.
I catch him from the corner
of my eye avoiding me,

his slips pursed with regret.
'Do you mind they all say you're miserable,
a byword for cod-depression?'

Showing me the back of my head
his fingers tremble on the hand-mirror,
his mouth open slightly as if caught

in revelation, the radio busy now
with The Carpenters,
and rain mysteriously clearing,

like fog lifting from a harbour
or a woman's back, her dress
sliding without hurry to the floor.

PART-TIMER

He gets here always on time — just —
wearing a smile not a sack like the rest of us.

We find him reading books in the library
and, worse, writing. Seriously,

how can we take him? Those educated vowels
and that stoop; that ever-so-careful

pause holding doors. Doesn't do playground,
doesn't stay for meetings, doesn't know he's born.

Ask him to show you his file and all you get
is a grin. Try him for lesson plans: he forgets.

Won't come to the pub and can't be arsed with lunch.
Says like he totally means it we're a *great bunch*

to work with. Is it us or is he taking the piss?
No, nowhere else. You've got me all to yourselves.

On the second day of the clear-out we find
a stack of them, enough for a class of forty,
reprinted since the fifties, their black jackets
and wraparound thin red line, like the equator,
a masterpiece of old world understatement.

At coffee they get taken outside, and by lunch
the empty corridors and assembly hall
ring to us trying to outquote each other
with camp invocations to *think carefully*
and describe the frolics of the wind.

They have to go in to the skip, we all know that,
but for weeks after small chunks appear
in the staff room, edging out the caption competition
and even the Lottery news as we struggle
to unearth its best worst paragraph.

By half term no one bothers to finish the story
which begins *Mother spread the tablecloth.*
Dad lit the primus stove. I carried the hamper.
Titty bounced around excitedly; or correct
The german was so tinny the scientist needed a microbe to see it.

We'll never find out now if father punched the burglar
in his sitting room, if there are proper adjectives
to describe the poor children from Africa,
or whatever happened to that class travelling by train
when Bloggs pulled the communication cord.

so he put it in the bin.
But if I leave it there
things could get sticky.
He carried it outside
and started to dig a hole.
Up to his waist in earth
he changed his mind again:
he'd heard stories of things like this
getting into the water table.
He looked at his watch.
An hour before they got home.
So why he found himself driving past the dump,
out of town, towards the fields,
he had no clue.
He took the second turn off the trunk road
and the third turn off the track off that.
He stopped at the first farm he came to
and went up to the door.
When no-one answered he knew he was home.
He was just lifting it out of the boot
when a voice exploded across the farmyard.
He had no option but to stick the farmer
in the container as well,
only with all the liquid, he wouldn't fit,
unless he could lose the legs.
It was becoming a problem.

HIS TRAINING FOR THE MISSION FIELD REMEMBERED

We were all crazy or stupid.
Some of us got out alive, many escaped
only with their addictions.

Those in the female population
were lucky if they left
without being stabbed.

The Masters were all drunkards or saints.
Or queer.
Chapel was four times daily.

We warmed the older boys' beds
by lying in them, naked,
and farting.

Beatings were frequent and public.
One boy drowned himself in the swimming pool in December.
The water was black and full of leaves.

Sport was a frozen leather ball with razors.
In summer there were dunkings in the brook
though — unofficially — they took place all year round.

Those who survived rarely speak,
even in letters.
By 'female population' I mean girls.

ON LUST

I have been reading Q's thesis in the library
and what a load of old rubbish it is.

Did Bordieu change nappies? —
I think we should be told.

Outside, the tennis court having it first haircut,
the groundsman bent feudally at his shadow.

Bourgeois? But of course:
last night we sat on the floor

eating meatballs with penne
in front of the Simpsons,

what I call family life.
Before thrashing them to sleep

I kiss them, obviously, twice,
my mother taught me everything.

The semiotics section is the only place,
all the best labels, plus the giggling sweet-eaters.

Was Eliot right about breasts?
I think he was. (I think he was.)

HELP

A chill day in the garden with the kids.
Do you want me to go on?

Me neither, but I think we all know by now
I'm not here to help you.

They made mudpies and I weeded.
Dug. Weeded. Whatever.

Are they the same? —
ask my brambles.

On my List Of Things To Do is the lawn
and so is starting a list.

Will I always be like this?
Of course, it's your father, says my mother

as if *that* explains everything.
How marvellous to be told you are useless

in a study overlooking the rose garden.
(I made that last bit up.)

Already they know about green fingers
and tiny seeds growing *bigger as the sky*.

That's not to say they won't mess up
like I have:

we chose their godparents well.
If I kept the best wine till last

it was an accident.
If I do sound tired, I am.

LATE AUGUST FRAGMENT

Autumn but not autumn, summer
but not. Tomorrow is a new sunrise

but for now I watch the struggle
of four beautiful Kenyans

round the 3,000m steeplechase in Seville,
one of whom will become immortal

before the night is through.
Yesterday, when everything seemed possible,

I cut myself shaving, and bled a little.
'I have no confidence in these matters

but am willing to pursue the dream,'
Cassirer doesn't say, and I agree.

Downstairs the etc etc and ER
being moving without me.

I am missing it just to be with *you*.
Who've I listened to recently? Fears,

certainly, the impossible bumblebee of truth
circling and circling me like death.

I am writing this to stay alive, by the way,
not the other way round.

POST-OP

Happy because I am here, not there,
opposite Frank Tyson's namesake recounting
demob from the RAF, getting bowling hints
in a ward the former guest wing of a duke;
South African Ingrid who called me dear, darling,
brought me Marmite when I asked for honey
and touched my arm, Jane from 'Nin-Zid',
Mr Wilson to her, sorry to always get to me last,
and Monica who said she'd look out for my book,
to have escaped smiling, woken up on morphine,
tried some passable pork casserole whose fault it wasn't
I vomited and more Radio 4, half asleep,
than I remember — though when you ask me news
out it all comes verbatim: a journalist shot dead
in Tyrone, the same, only captured without a passport
on the Afghan border, and more reaction to Berlusconi:
how the world outside goes on, like after birth,
without knowing how drôle I was going under.

'2 BECOME 1'

In the newly-opened Virgin
there's a video playing *Lady*
and the Tramp, silently, incongruous
with *This is Hardcore*: we join
it at the moment when the Tramp
leads the dog-catcher a merry
dance over and back a three
foot fence, the chase leading him
as we know to 'Snob Hill' or, as the Bulldog
with the 'gor-blimey accent has it
later 'Miss Park Avenue 'erself.'
You know by now this is my way
of saying sorry for having no money,
by spending money on something
we don't need and are only 60%
certain we like. 'I don't know
what it's called,' I stumble, before
delivering it, note-perfect, to the smiling
assistant and queue of one goth and two
truanting nine-year olds, red
with embarrassment: 'It's for a friend.'

PARENTHOOD

after Theodore Roethke

I have known the inexorable sadness of children's shoes,
squat in their boxes, scuffed after five minutes' wearing,
the incalculable tristesse of Thomas the Tank Engine slippers,
DayGlo blue nylon with immutable plastic badges,
and the cost of all this which is sleeplessness, vomit and Dettox spray,
rage of shoelace tying,
bottom wiping, yoghurt scraping, Ribena mopping,
as you try, one hand glued to your hair, your mouth burning
with sores, to speak politely on the telephone
to the woman who is buying your house,
the doctor who says don't bend, the friend who is just back from Prague
your mother who begins 'Well, in my day...
And I have seen dust collect under their beds, there is nothing
I can do to prevent it, visions of gin, gallons of it, before breakfast,
incomprehensible gobbledegook of Tommee Tippee instructions,
Tixylix, dawn-light of Calpol, poignancy of vests in their packets,
blockage of buggies in swing doors
and heartbreak of stories by the fire,
Granpa, *Peepo!*, *Peace at Last*, the firelight wavering
and breathing slowing to a pulse
that overcomes you with drowsiness,
the furies of your life ebbing as the story, here, now, unfurls,
grows, is fixed, not a word omitted or changed,
by stories are we known and do tell ourselves, Daddy,
I'm tired now please, carry me, you forgot vitamins, to bed.

ERRAND

Behind, my children, my life.
The bakery is open.

A man is laying crates of bread,
one on top of the other,
in the boot of a waiting car.

The newspaper boy wobbles on his bike.

Walking back, I tuck the loaf
under my arm, my hand cupped
round it. At school we carried
rugby balls the same way.

It left the other hand free
for punching friends and enemies
as they sauntered past.

I TRY NOT TO SHOUT AT THEM

but I do: breakfast, bedtimes,
after a glass of Chardonnay —
I am not fussy. They run off
laughing, pretending not to be hurt,
then I shout some more.

Stepping on Lego is a good one,
so is spilt apple juice. During *Cold Feet*
they do not even get eye contact.
In the morning I say *No you can't
use my lip salve, you'll only break it*.

FEBRUARY

It is not cold.
And isn't this freedom,
to sit here on a Sunday
having got up at six,
dosed him with milk,
made tea, flicked through
yesterday's *Independent*
and now to be plucking
black grapes from a white
bowl, listening to the fridge
shiver and settle and reminding
myself that hum is the fan-
oven defrosting chicken
breasts which later I will
cook in the traditional
manner with the radio,
garlic and bacon. I did
so want today to be happy.

THE TIMES

05:00 hours is bad and anything with a three in it,
for example 03:13. Those times between 02:00 and 04:00
are crippling for the next day's decisions as are those times
on a Sunday and most times during the ravages of February.
Unspeakable times include 04:59 and 01:07 — but for some reason
05:58 is not a bad time, unlike its cousins 01:58 and 02:58
who are total buggers and always will be. Among the joke-times
are anything before midnight, the lucid moments just after midnight
and those just after making love, with sleep approaching.

The why-even-bother-times are as follows: 06:14, 06:27, 06:32
and the infrequently-mentioned 06:02. The I-want to-die-now-times
list 02:09, 04:11 and 03:33. The fact we all go on living regardless
must point to something, the resilience of the human spirit, perhaps,
equality of opportunity for fathers, or even Japanese alarm clock reliability.
However, my familiarity with 04:19 of late has wrenched the bottom
drawer from my desk and scattered the contents blowing across the park
to be laughed at by children and dogs. I find this is inducing in me
a quite serious indifference to most subjects, even my work.

THE DIFFERENCE
for Jim

The lives we're living,
what difference do they make?

We wake up,
throw our children in the air
and catch them laughing
into our arms.

Friends come and go, seasons pass,
the leaves collect silently
in the garden.

Which reminds me,
there's pruning to be done
and bonfires to build.

What is it that we're doing
in this world to make it better,
a place more easy to wake in
for our children?

In the middle of all this
I am amazed
the sun still finds time
to rise beautifully over these roofs
and never asks anything in return.

THE SCHOOL-WALK

They hop down the path, pausing
to kick crab-apples, but terrified
of stepping on one. Then out through
the gate and before it clacks shut
they're off on the ten-second, headlong
sprint down the hill, till they collapse,
gasping theatrically on the low wall
by the language-school steps. Instead
of cajoling them up (it took me
two terms to learn this) I march past
to wait at the corner where no one
indicates left, seventy yards from home,
easily our most dangerous moment.
Then Dog Poo Alley, their favourite,
clean the last few weeks, almost disappointing;
past Jon-the-curate's house; over the cul-de-sac
where Liz has just moved in,
next door to the Labour-voting
skin specialist Mandy says is selling up
because he has too much space. We pick
our way through the traffic and the rest is straight.
The Royal Deaf School playing field tries to shine
in the morning's first attempt at sun
as Merenna sings 'Straw Belly Fields'
at top volume making the lollipop lady smile
an instant, the traffic parted like an ocean
and us still looking forward to the other side.

III

FROM HOW FAR FROM HERE IS HOME?

Leaving home is a kind of forgiveness
— Garrison Keillor

WE HAD GONE TO THE AIRPORT TO GET HER

and sat chewing microwaved beef in the restaurant.
We were discussing the possibilities

of me getting a job: 'Well, what do you think?'
Underneath I saw a policeman pass

With a gun in his hand. 'I think you're right,
that something is better than nothing –

but I won't do *anything*.' He had taken
the day off especially to meet her

and I had driven, to get more practice.
Later I heard them kissing in the hall:

'Thank you for loving me';
'Thank you for coming back to me.'

She pulled presents from her suitcase.
Liqueurs, handkerchiefs and a book

of black and white photographs for my brother.
And for me some writing paper, the kind I very much liked using.

GRANDPAPA

In Memoriam Marcel Robert, 1899-1977

You were plum tree blossom and mothball smells,
black braces on a white shirt, and anger

that might at any moment explode
into the utmost care.

You tended your garden
with your watchmaker's precision,

fighting all your life with your heart,
the ticker you couldn't rely on.

Your only word of English was *Goodbye*
followed by a laugh rasping on itself

blunting the joke we couldn't see.
To greet us you pinched our cheeks

as if squeezing us into speech
then your hard, just-shaved kiss

which sighed as your head bent near us.
We learned *Bonjour, Merci, S'il-te-plait?,*

Bonne nuit and *Dors bien*; to break our bread
with our hands, and to sip black tea.

It was on your last holiday with us when we talked,
a hot Cornish fortnight where you ordered cream

every day. Our tongues unmoored themselves
the time we fished for mackerel,

you, a mountain-man and us,
wide-eyed from the suburbs.

You still caught the most,
as you shrugged with that wheezy laugh,

delighted to ride your luck,
a perfectionist visited by chance.

it was gravy, all of it — your grandchildren
growing; sea breezes spooning the air you craved;

and your straw hat sunning itself,
bleaching to its small, obstinate rim.

LOVE

The hush of a Test at Lords
and slow applause from a boundary.

'There's one worse thing than England doing badly
and that's them doing well.'

Its enmities suited you fine,
its pauses, the gravity of its humour.

I found you peering mole-like into the screen,
your old tie faithful to occasion.

'Some people call it rhubarb and custard
but I prefer egg and bacon.'

We'd play it out afterwards in the garden:
you someone I had never heard of

and me some new bod seeking to impress.
I never got near the balls you spun me

googly after googly eluding me
like the grin at the end of your run

cooking up something fresh.
Stumped by your absence,

bowled clean by your love not coming back,
it's you I grope for now,

imagining the long future without you,
improving my action, cursing my technique.

ELEGY FOR MIKE MULVANEY

The day I introduced you to the class
you prompted me with this whisper:
'Mike. Let them call me Mike.'

I loved your ex-Head's humility,
your prop forward's shoulders
and neck bending to dislodge

the mask of authority.
You saw through everyone:
parents, children and teachers;

how power was really a triangle
equal on all sides, was a song,
not a system, of grace.

Yet afterwards you told me:
'Education's a mess.'
To do that, to speak and not care

what others thought, might serve
as your epitaph. More resonant,
though, is this, from the only book

you gave me, underlined and scored
by your impatient hand. *Democracy*
has slipped through their fingers.

And, next door in the margin,
your own SO WE MUST GIVE IT BACK.

SCHOOL PHOTOGRAPH

I am the one on the left.
The one you notice, but don't,
amongst the four hundred
identically grey dots grinning
themselves into posterity
this chill April morning.

Top corner, back row.
Jackson is wobbling on my left,
on my right the ten feet drop.
I grit my smirk till it hurts
and think of far away where
this instant will fade in the study.

I can picture my parents.
For whom school is this sepia
negative glimpsed fondly
in the sunlight over sherry.
That's me, there, I will say to them.
What do you think?

Probably it will be *Very nice*
but I know deep down my smile
will never be ready. To hang me
will cost them even more.
And without it my life's incomplete.
This is it. The moment we've waited for.

Click. Except it does not go click.
It goes whirr, panning round us
like a gun, very carefully.
Soon it will all be over.
The geography master is bald.
I can see the river from here.

PAY

Went into it after the Sixties.
All you needed then was two A levels
a guitar and some energy
and you'd be a Head after six years.

Those were the days.
Class sizes where you actually
knew the kids' names.
Ideals. The belief that somehow

it mattered. Pay that wasn't a joke.
Left it after some aggro
with a fourth former
the year I got married.

He was asking for it.
The Head quite good as it turned out.
He said that personally he liked me.
By the time I came back

it'd changed. Paperwork for breakfast,
formula funding. Thirty eight to a class.
No more blackboards either.
Down to the Arms at half time

to drown a few then back
to the little buggers. Discipline
I give them. All that shit
about relevance. I'm home

by half four. One day I'll leave.
Not like it was before.
I think that's right, yes.
I think they should suffer.

The first thing is to read the poem several times.
That way you become familiar with the text.
Not one study guide ever published can replace
the virtue of *the words themselves*. Make notes

as you go along, in the margin. Underline things.
Write down what succeeds. Analyse the poet's
technique. Is it rhymed and does it have metre?
Does it correspond to a pattern, *abab*, for example,

or a sonnet? If not, is it free verse, or *vers libre*?
Form is all very well but if it's not married to content
the poem will fail as Art. Then to the actual material.
Take the nouns. Are they solid – or abstract?

Door is of the solid kind, *fear* of the abstract.
Thus, a poem about a door might really be about
fear. Watch out for this. It is called imagery.
Then take a look at the verbs. The verbs

are a poem's engine. Do they push the poem along
or do they hold it back? Also, the adjectives.
An adjective must work like a muscle, very hard.
If it doesn't, it shouldn't be there. A poem which

contains the word *nice*, for example, is nearly always
bad. Finally, what is the poem about? Does it
contain nudity, or references to young boys?
How is the poet using them, to explore his feelings,

or does he have other ideas? If blackmail
is involved it's possible the poem is in code.
Anyone with problems in this area should see me
afterwards. The door to my study's never closed.

HIDING

I hide mostly if I can.
That's me with the invisible smile.
Over there.   It's good since the class
got so big, it means I can hide
anywhere I want. I like hiding.

Miss kept me in the other day.
Lunchtime, the noises from the playground.
Me, on my own, with her. Nowhere
to hide then. Her face creased
with concern. You will tell, won't you,

she beamed. If anyone does anything
that you don't like. Like touching.
I nodded and said I would. Anything
so I could go out to hide. First time
she spoke to me this term.

She's nice really. Doesn't shout.
Doesn't hit. It's good. On Friday we
have P.E. and she lets me carry the ball.
I make sure when we change
that I don't make any false moves

or she'll know. Rubbing is louder
than words. Looking louder still.
I like this top, it's got long sleeves.
Then back to the class to hide,
hiding in my head, by the pencils.

THE MAN NEXT DOOR

is bluff, calls me Mate, My Friend.
A builder, his van splutters each morning as he goes.
He is on his second wife.

His children rumble about his house
and he swears at them, makes them cry.
None of this seems to wear him down.

Once I saw him standing in the street, barefoot,
stripped to his jeans. He was pink
as a baby and his muscles shone.

If I were in trouble in any way
he'd be the first to offer help,
a break-in, a job that needed doing.

His daughter comes home late from school
and he jumps down the steps to meet her.
He bends down to kiss her very softly, on the forehead.

A JOGGER

His life is a dedication
to the hatred of meat.
His grimace is a space-
saving video. His muscles
are psychology graduates,
his watch the crack
of a firing squad. His wife
is a cordless phone, his sex
is a milestone of pain.
His sweat is beyond
reproach. His credit card
makes gifts to minorities.
Bleach goes swimming
in his eyes, his soles whisper
threats to the tarmac.
His rucksack pushes him
forward, inflating him like a sail.

THE MEN'S GROUP IN THE ANTENATAL CLASS
for Lucy Markes

Beached on an oatmeal floor
we are five distracted Buddhas
offering bad football commentaries
on 'The Pros and Cons of Pregnancy'.

On our page of two halves 'Feeling
sick as a parrot (for her)' is
mirrored by 'Practising bedtime stories';
'Stress' by 'Big sense of achievement'.

Another name for all this could be 'The
subtle avoidance of eye contact', or
'Trying not to think about sex'.
In the report-back afterwards

we are praised for *not* writing down
'She does all the driving these days,
so I'm free to get pissed at parties'.
Which side? One of us whispers. *Pro — or con?*

THE LODGERS

They have friends who phone up at midnight.
They fry garlic with the kitchen door open.

They burn toast. They print circles on the floor
with milk bottles, uncertain of where they belong.

They receive packets of forwarded mail, catalogues
of horror comics, brochures for forthcoming jazz

at the Barbican. They disappear on the weekends.
They reappear, ravenous, and use all the saucepans.

They scan the television pages. They learn how to
programme the video. They rediscover baked beans.

Over breakfast they analyse fox hunting.
They do three week's washing in a day.

They do not worry. They change the radio tuning
and do not change it back. They are absent

from Town Hall records. Their job is to hoover
the stairs. They smile. They live in our house.

BASIL AND CHOPPED TOMATOES

Too many [poems] seemed to be about cutting up
basil and tomatoes while Mozart played.
Liz Lochhead, *The Observer*, 13/3/94.

There are too many poems
with basil and chopped tomatoes
in them. This will not be
one of them. Nor will Mozart

play in the background, nor soft
breezes delicately waft through
the kitchen. Probably it will
be Desert Island Discs

and chicken casserole while you read
the Sunday papers. We do not
have a cat so the cat will not
appear, hungrily. The baby —

is the baby allowed to be present?
It will be its first week
of sitting up on its own in
the playpen. If not it will be crying.

The poem is almost completed
but one feels it lacks imagery.
Ever dropped a tin of tomatoes
onto a hot pan of garlic

and chillies in extra virgin oil?
You don't need a poet to help you.
If you get the timing just right
it sounds like a round of applause.

AFTER LOVE

'When this is all over…,' we said,
and laughed and made that bed;
made other things seem trivial and unenduring,
lying there joking and seeming

equal. Yet so often now we are like strangers
guilty of acts committed in darkness.
Preferring not to talk we notice
how uneven the body is

in sleep and lie and listen to thoughts
which have no hope of finding voice,
even in these moments
after love, after everything is done, less tense.

Outside the clouds are vacant, lost,
at random. As we turn and shift to rest
with slow and separate movements
the wind bleats at our door, sounding human.

HERE

for Tatiana

We live here now and everything is going to be fine.
We have a new bed, and more gifts
than we know what to do with.

The car starts first time each morning
and in the evening we cook together
and are easy, two friends.

People show kindness in unmerited ways,
with words and with flowers.
Our neighbours recognise us, and smile.

We drink out of bowls
and we eat off a table that shines.
We have made this and this is our home.

We live here now and everything is going to be fine.

BY THE SAME AUTHOR

How Far From Here Is Home?

The Difference

Nowhere Better Than This

Economical, witty and observant. An habitual and natural delicacy covers the more primitive emotions that thrive beneath the Carver-like surface.

Marita Over, *Ambit*

In both style and content a mix of casual and formal. All the poems feel genuinely personal. Anthony Wilson's poetry has an easy-going surface but a thoughtful interior.

Paul Munden, *The North*

Anthony Wilson's acute and astute observations are witty, humorous and often poignant. He looks at what it means to occupy various roles as son, brother, father, husband, teacher —and the best of these poems create a finely balanced tension, tantalizing, resonant.

Catherine Smith, *The Frogmore Papers*

Worple Press is an independent publishing house that specialises in poetry, art and alternative titles.

Worple Press can be contacted at:
PO Box 328, Tonbridge, Kent TN9 1WR Tel 01732 368 958
email: theworpleco@aol.com.

Trade orders: Central Books, 99 Wallis Road, London E9 5LN
Tel 0845 4589911

TITLES INCLUDE:

Against Gravity – **Beverley Brie Brahic**
(A5 Price £8.00 ISBN 1-905208-03-0, pp 72)

Sailing to Hokkaido – **Joseph Woods**
(A5 Price £6.00 ISBN 0 9530947-6-6, pp 60)

Bearings – **Joseph Woods**
(A5 Price £8.00 / 10 Euros ISBN 1905208-00-6, pp 64)

'his work shows an impressive reach and range' *Eiléan Ní Chuilleanáin*

'good and interesting poems well-presented' *Books Ireland*

A Ruskin Alphabet - **Kevin Jackson**
(A6 Price £4.50 ISBN 0 9530947-2-3, pp. 88)
'you may like to consult *A Ruskin Alphabet* by Kevin Jackson, a collection of facts and opinions on ruskin and Ruskinites, together with a variety of pithy remarks from the man himself' *TLS*

Looking In All Directions – **Peter Kane Dufault**
(A5 Price £10.00 ISBN 0 9530947-5-8, pp. 188)

'Wonderful stuff'   *Ted Hughes*

The Great Friend and Other Translated Poems – **Peter Robinson**
(A5 Price £8.00 ISBN 0-9530947-7-4, pp. 75)
Poetry Book Society Recommended Translation

The Verbals – **Kevin Jackson in Conversation with Iain Sinclair** (A5 Price £12.00 / 20 Euros ISBN 0-9530947-9-0, pp. 148)

'Highly interesting.' *The Guardian*
'Cultists will be eager to get their hands on it.' *TLS*
'Worple Press have done it again... this sparkling introduction to Sinclair and his world.'   *The Use of English*

Stigmata – **Clive Wilmer**
(A5 Price £10.00 / 15 Euros ISBN 1-905208-01-4, pp. 28)

'a brilliant piece of work which brings honour to our time'
Sebastian Barker

FORTHCOMING TITLES

Buried At Sea — **poems by Iain Sinclair**

Bowl — **first collection from Elizabeth Cook**

To be In the Same World — **Peter Kane Dufault**

Warp and Weft — **an anthology of Worple writing**